ARTHUR H

1819-1861

First published in 2001 by
Short Books
15 Highbury Terrace
London N5 1UP

A CIP catalogue record for this book
is available from the British Library.

ISBN 0 571 20815 0

Printed in Great Britain by
Bookmarque Ltd, Croydon, Surrey

THE VOICE OF VICTORIAN SEX

Arthur H Clough
1819-1861

RUPERT CHRISTIANSEN

✳ SHORT BOOKS

To Bill and Virginia Nicholson, and
the nurturing spirit of Court House

IN 1941, AT THE CLIMAX of a radio broadcast celebrating Roosevelt's commitment to the fight against Hitler, Winston Churchill quoted some inspirational lines:

> And not by eastern windows only,
> When daylight comes, comes in the light,
> In front the sun climbs slow, how slowly,
> But westward, look, the land is bright.

This is the final verse of Arthur Hugh Clough's 'Say Not the Struggle Naught Availeth', a brief poem well known to Churchill's generation, probably written during the French siege of Mazzini's short-lived Roman republic in 1849. Its appeal to the Age of Empire is not hard to understand. Ladies could admire its Shelleyan radiance; militants and believers liked the way it preaches steadfastness in times of trouble and promises the dawn of hope – injunctions as morally uplifting as anything in Kipling's 'Recessional' or 'If…'. With an isolated, beleaguered Britain gazing across the Atlantic and glimpsing the prospect of American salvation, the matching of those lines to that moment was a rhetorical masterstroke.

But Clough, I think, would have been embarrassed by his sudden elevation to the spotlight of history; and since that broadcast he seems to have crept back into the shadows of the literary second-rank. Today, he is not widely read and is only sometimes in print. His verse is rarely set for exams or syllabuses, and features scantily in anthologies (usually nothing more than 'Say Not the Struggle' and his satirical rewriting of the Ten Commandments, 'The Latest Decalogue'). Nor has he benefited from the current obsession with biography – the last full-length study appeared over 30 years ago. In the course of writing this essay, I have discovered that inasmuch as anyone has heard of him at all, he is vaguely recalled as either the wunderkind of Dr Arnold's Rugby who never fulfilled his youthful promise and ended up wrapping parcels for Florence Nightingale – a picture drawn from the brief, sharp caricature which appears in Lytton Strachey's brilliant but misleading *Eminent Victorians* – or as one of that rather unappealing band of 19th-century intellectuals trapped by what Clough's friend Matthew Arnold called 'the melancholy, long, withdrawing roar' of the ebbing tide of Christian faith.

Even his contemporaries struck a negative note: only years after his premature death at the age of 42 in 1861, he was being commemorated, with a fond sigh, as a pathetic failure. 'He certainly had great genius', admitted his friend and Oxford contemporary Benjamin Jowett, 'but some want of will or some want of harmony with things around him prevented his creating anything worthy of himself.' That view was general.

But what sort of life constitutes a failure? Where does the disappointment lie, and what would have been worthy of him? After all, Clough was a fond husband, a loving father, a loyal and warm friend. By the age of 30, he had written two of the most readable and intelligent long poems in the English language: 'The Bothie of Tober-na-Vuolich' and 'Amours de Voyage'; later, he also made a sterling contribution, of far more significance than Strachey suggests, to Florence Nightingale's revolutionary report on *Matters Affecting the Health, Efficiency and Hospital Administration of the British Army*. If this is failure, it is failure of a somewhat Olympian kind.

Clough should be of great interest to us now. He is the most modern of Victorian poets. In terms of everything from his attitude to metre to his sceptical moral temper, he is far closer to our own cultural persuasion than Tennyson or Browning. As his friend JA Froude put it, he wanted 'to let the uncertainties remain uncertain'. The atypical 'Say Not the Struggle' aside, most of what he wrote is profoundly liberal-minded and irreverent of pomp and politics. His verse does not sing or soar or rhapsodise: it is prosy, anxious, witty, multivalent, and it delves into matters of sexual instinct with a startling frankness and sensuality unparalleled in 19th-century English literature. Biographers of the past have tended to dwell on his struggle with Christianity, but, from our own perspective, one can see that his struggle to relate to women was even more problematic. This has also been perhaps the most neglected aspect of Clough's biography, and what follows will therefore highlight it.

***

Clough's is not, alas, a richly documented life. Although two volumes of his letters run to over 500 pages, he was not a forthcoming, confessional or even particularly entertaining correspondent, and the evidence relating to various crucial episodes is fragmentary – how one longs to know more about his collaboration with Florence Nightingale, for example. But we are fortunate to have a clear picture of the small boy painted by his younger sister Anne Jemima, herself distinguished after her brother's death as a pioneer of women's university education.

On his father's side Arthur Hugh Clough came from the well-established Tory squirearchy – Sir Richard Clough had worked with the Elizabethan financial wizard Sir Thomas Gresham, and until the late 18th century his descendants owned and farmed substantial tracts of land on the Welsh Borders. Dr Johnson's great friend Mrs

Thrale was a scion, and the family's one egregious literary connection. In the early 19th century, however, the estate's fortunes waned as the result of a bank crash, and Clough's father James set up as a cotton merchant in Liverpool, where he married Ann Perfect, the daughter of a Yorkshire banker. James Clough was a kindly man, too sanguine and easy-going to be successful in trade; his wife was made of sterner stuff, a woman (so her daughter recalled) of an Evangelical bent and 'stern integrity' who 'cared little for general society… loved what was grand, noble and enterprising', but was also 'critical and hard to please… laughing unmercifully at the weaknesses of her friends and relations'. She gave birth to four children of whom the second was Arthur Hugh, born on 1 January 1819.

Three years later James Clough's business interests took him and his family to Charleston, South Carolina, a centre of the cotton industry. Here, in a large, ugly red-brick house by the sea, Arthur grew into 'a somewhat grave and studious boy, not without tastes for walking, shooting and sight-seeing, but with little capacity for play and mixing with others'. A streak of obstinacy also manifested itself, as in his fastidious refusal to take off his shoes and paddle on the exotic sands of Sullivan's Island, where the family spent their summer vacations: even when pubescent, he could only be impelled to act from his own choice, and would not follow what others did. But the most significant episode in what seems to have been a relatively secure and happy childhood was the year that James Clough was summoned back to England.

'Then Arthur became my mother's constant companion,' remembered Anne Jemima, known as Annie. 'Though then only just seven, he was always considered as the genius of our family. He was a beautiful boy, with soft, silky, almost black hair, and shining dark eyes, and a small delicate mouth, which our nurse was so afraid of spoiling when he was a baby that she insisted on getting a tiny spoon for his special use.' In her husband's absence, Ann Clough 'poured out her heart' to Arthur, and 'they read much together' – perhaps something of an emotional burden to a sensitive seven-year-old.

In 1828 the Cloughs returned to England and deposited the nine-year-old Arthur at a boarding school in Chester with his elder brother Charles, an uncle was put *in loco parentis*. His first letters home to Charleston are solemn and stoical: 'I am happy to acknowledge the receipt of mama's letter to Charles, which arrived here on the 8th, on which day we went out to the Miss Foulkes's, to whom we presented her compliments and desired us to send theirs to her when we wrote next to any of you…' If he felt abandoned or betrayed, he certainly did not show it.

A year later, he moved on to one of the oldest public

schools, Rugby, where a new Headmaster Dr Thomas Arnold had just begun a remarkable educational experiment. Like all such institutions, Rugby was little short of anarchic. Drunkenness, thieving and violent bullying were endemic, with flogging or expulsion as the only means of discipline. Lessons were confined to a narrow curriculum of scripture, classics and mathematics; once they were over, pupils were virtually abandoned to their own devices. At night, herded into boarding houses owned by helpless 'dames', they were locked into filthy dormitories where they slept as many as six to a bed (a single bed being available only by expensive supplementary payment to the termly fees). Moralists had long recognised all this as a scandal, but not until Arnold did anyone dare grapple with its iniquity.

A young intellectual, deeply read in the ideas of Coleridge and German biblical criticism, Arnold aimed at nothing less than the moral reform of the entire nation. Christian principles should inform all branches of society, he thought, but this would be achieved by attention to the ethical heart of Jesus' teaching rather than quibbles over doctrinal detail or insistence on ritual and hierarchy. The Church of England should embrace the broadest possible range of sects and denominations, and wake up to contemporary realities. Monasticism and meditation were all very well, but it was action that was needed:

British society was in a terrible state, the aristocracy corrupt and cynical, the middle class rudderless, the lower orders hungry and depraved. The Ten Commandments should be rewritten; the state should take responsibility for education, on the Napoleonic model; restrictions on Roman Catholics should be lifted; foreign colonisation, with its wonderful opportunities to build enlightened new communities, ought to be encouraged; and the proto-socialist idea that wealth should be redistributed was not an altogether bad one. There was, in other words, much to be done – and where better to start than on the template of a school, dedicated to the training of a new elite of leaders?

Arnold was not only a visionary, he was also sternly practical, and his revolution at Rugby was executed with impeccable detail. The number of pupils was limited to a governable 300. Fees were raised to pay for improvements, including higher salaries for staff. Single beds became the norm, in houses administered by male teachers overseeing a cadre of trusted sixth-form seniors, known after the Roman fashion as Prefects. Whenever a flag flew outside the Headmaster's office, any member of the school could feel free to call in and discuss any problem. The curriculum was made more 'relevant' by the incorporation of modern languages and history, with prizes awarded for outstanding effort and achievement.

Debates and productions of suitable classical plays filled spare time; manly outdoor exercise of a spartan kind was also encouraged (the vogue for competitive team sports was as yet a generation off).

Arnold's dearest hope was not to cram information into callow brains or to create a breed of super-scholars but to tame the animal boy into a Christian gentleman. To that end he established a benevolently, if intensely, supervised environment in which there existed firm and impenetrable barriers between virtue and vice. '*Orando, laborando*', 'By praying, by working', became the school's new motto, aptly summarising its new ethos. Arnold disliked flogging miscreants: shame was his preferred weapon, an appeal to the conscience. Every Sunday, he delivered a sermon to the assembled school – for Arnold insisted on being Chaplain as well as Headmaster – and this was the linchpin of his strategy. Never more than 20 minutes long, always grippingly narrated and couched 'in the language of common life and applied to the cases of common life', his orations electrified impressionable minds, 'and so, wearily and little by little' – in the words of Thomas Hughes, the author of *Tom Brown's Schooldays*, an encomium to Arnold's Rugby in novelistic form – it was 'brought home to the young boy, for the first time, the meaning of his life: that it was no fool's or sluggard's paradise into which he had wandered by chance, but a battlefield ordained from of old, where there are no spectators, but the youngest must take his side, and the stakes are life and death'.

Ten-year-old Arthur Hugh Clough was ripe for the plucking. Bereft of his closest family, clever, determined yet introspective, he was Rugby's perfect laboratory guinea-pig and duly swallowed the medicine. Arnold watched over him lovingly, and during vacations took the lad to the Lake District with his own sons; Mrs Arnold provided the missing motherly attentions. No wonder that the school became Clough's emotional home, and in some sense remained so for the rest of his life. Throughout his eight years there, 'Tom Yankee' (as he was nicknamed) shone as the golden boy. He won prizes, he led the Prefects as head of School House, he was a keen athlete and swimmer, as well as a superb goalkeeper in the furious, chaotic games of football which preceded the development of the sport to which the school gave its name.

He also began to write, though never with any overwhelming compulsion or evidence of remarkable talent: his first surviving poem, penned at the age of 11 and commemorating the death of George IV, is the sort of doggerel that any bright child could have produced:

O Muse of Britain teach me how to sing
In verses sad of our late, noble King.

Teach me in notes of sorrow to proclaim
To all the world our noble Prince's fame.

And even his later adolescent contributions to *The Rugby
Magazine* are no more than awkwardly pretentious and
flat-footed. It was the responsibility of editing this pub-
lication – another of Arnold's innovations – which seems
to have engaged and exercised him more, simply because
'responsibility' was such a crucially charged word in
Arnold's vocabulary. Although its pages contain a good
deal of heavy-handed schoolboy facetiousness ('bravo',
'bravissimo' and 'pshaw' are favourite exclamations), the
underlying tone of *The Rugby Magazine* is always
missionary. 'Did I say that our motive was to give amusement and knowledge?' Clough asks parsonically in an
editorial. 'Our motive, we trust, is a higher one. It is one
of love and gratitude; it is to pay our debt to the mother
that has fostered, and is fostering, our young intellects;
nor, we trust, our intellects alone; it is to raise her still
higher than she is raised, or at least to maintain her on her
present elevation.'

And therein lay the trouble. Rugby was too relentlessly
earnest; it made, indeed, a Jesuit seminary seem like a
funfair, and even Victorians saw that its idealism could
damage tender psyches. Reviewing Clough's achievement
shortly after his death, Walter Bagehot wisely noted that

'a susceptible, serious, intellectual boy may be injured by the incessant inculcation of the awfulness of life and the magnitude of great problems.' Clough, he believed, 'required quite another sort of teaching' from the sort he received from Arnold – 'to be told to take things easily; not to try to be wise overmuch [and] to go on living quietly and obviously, and to see what truth should come to him'.

In fact, the adult Clough would be desperately aware of the corrosive effects of what he called his 'almost animal irritability of conscience', and, although he loyally never put his retrospective views of Arnold on record in his own voice, the prose epilogue to his dramatic poem 'Dipsychus' presents the character of a worldly and dyspeptic old uncle who does the job for him. 'What is the true purpose of education?' he asks. 'Simply to make plain to the young understanding the laws of the life they will have to enter. For example – that lying won't do, thieving still less; that if they are cowards the whole world will be against them; that if they will have their own way, they must fight for it. Etc. Etc.' For Rugby, such moral horse-sense was not enough: it demanded that teenagers look inside them-selves, root out the evil and strive for nothing less than a modern sort of sainthood.

Young Clough put what his sister recalled as 'intense interest and labour' into his 'moral work among the boys', and when he was seated next to Dr Arnold in the library, staring up at him 'with an almost feminine expression of trust and affection', he could feel optimistic that it was all worthwhile. A letter home expresses pride, for example, in the establishment of a sixth-form common room, its furnishing subsidised by the Headmaster to the tune of £5, where the prefects ate supper 'in the most gentlemanly fashion… with trays and knives, and we buy very good cheeses for ourselves occasionally, and make a very sociable meal of it'. Yet there were also times when the old anarchy broke out again and even Arnold himself was driven below his own exigent standards. In 1833, for instance, when Clough was 14, there had been a terrible incident when this paragon of Headmasters had accused another 14-year-old boy called March of lying to him. March protested his innocence, at which Arnold flew into one of his rare but terrifying rages and proceeded to give him a thrashing – 18 strokes, six more than any of his unregenerate birch-happy predecessors ever delivered. March had suffered from a hernia since infancy and spent the next two days in a state of total physical collapse until his parents arrived to remove him from the school. It then emerged that March had been telling the truth all along, a revelation which impelled Arnold to make a full and abject apology to the entire school. The story reached a local newspaper, and Arnold found himself publicly excoriated. Eight members of his staff wrote to defend his good name, and the scandal eventually died down.

The following year Clough reported 'a little fellow not more than 13 years old at the most' who was discovered 'quite drunk'; and in 1836 there was a brutal fight between two boys which resulted in one of them 'going mad from blows on the head from a leaded cane', fireworks being set off in the school yard, and Arnold lashing out when his attempt to control the situation rationally failed. In a school as exposed and experimental as Rugby, the stakes were so high, the exhortations so noble, that it was all too easy to fall short. For those who identified the Headmaster with God, it must have been confusing.

All the muddle is reflected in Clough's surviving diaries and letters of the period. As a senior member of the school, he takes its cares upon him and writes as though ventriloquising Arnold. He complains to his sister Annie that 'there is a deal of evil springing up in the School, and it is to be feared that the tares will choke much of the wheat'. Whatever good there was 'in the top of the school, it is what may be called disagreeable good, having much evil mixed with it, especially in little matters. So that from these persons I am trying to show that good is not necessarily disagreeable, that a Christian may be and is likely to be a gentleman'. In other words, good was not good enough; for Rugbeians, it had to be perfection.

Clough wasn't exactly smug, but he was certainly a prig: on himself he was even harder than he was on others. His scruples about editing *The Rugby Magazine* are positively comical. He worried about offending people whose contributions he rejected, and he worried about spending too much time on the task. He worried about the magazine failing, he worried about it succeeding. He even worried that the power he held might corrupt him. A graphologist would be fascinated by the way the handwriting in his diaries modulates, from neatly rounded copperplate to crazy lurching scrawl, as he beats his breast and tries to unknot the dilemmas.

He is sinful, oh so very sinful. 'I have been here a week and am in a miserable state of distrust on God's mercy,' he writes on returning to school after the holidays of 1836. 'I deserve to be made mad like [the poet] Cowper. May God forbid. I will still hope & pray. *Mens sana in corpore sano.* I do not feel at all inclined to sin willingly, but I have been a good deal in the state. O wretched man that I am.' What were these sins? Indolence, vanity ('an atmosphere of conceit around me enveloping my whole frame like the body does the soul'), a tendency to be indiscriminate in offering friendship, a tendency to the opposite, a tendency to indulge other sinners against whom he should draw a firm line. 'I do hope and pray that my heart is not the slave of these wicked feelings.'

He also worried that he competed too hard for worldly glory: 'How well I remember the night when I sat up till 12 to write out what I had composed that evening. That excitement I shall never forget. It was indeed rich & overpowering excitement. My head trembled with aching & my eyes were half-sealed up – but I went on – on – on till it was all done.' The unmistakably erotic rhythm of this suggests what probably underlay his hysteria. From 1833, Clough periodically marked his diary with a *, which seems to denote descents into masturbation, then an unspeakable vice thought to lead to insanity, degeneracy and damnation. 'Shame shame that there shd be any sensuality when I know full well the higher pleasures of intellect, yes, & those highest ones of Christianity,' he laments. Often occurring on the same pages as lists of his scriptural readings, the asterisks literally blot his copybook, glossing 'my old temptation', 'my worst temptation', 'senses of the body', 'the passion to which I have given way', 'visits to sin and wickedness'. 'Feel almost inclined to sin because it seems monotonous to be good all day', he writes at one teetering moment.

But good he was, and in 1837 he left Rugby in a blaze of *summa cum laude* and *phi beta kappa* glory, having won a scholarship to Balliol College, Oxford. On his departure, Arnold broke his normal practice to congratulate him before the entire school and every boy in the school is said to have queued up to shake his hand. Arnold wrote to Clough's father, thanking him for the gift of a boy who had 'passed eight years without a fault' and 'gone on ripening gradually in all excellence intellectual and spiritual'.

***

The move to Balliol was an obvious step for Clough: it was the Oxford college with the highest academic reputation of its day, and, although its political colour was Tory and royalist, it favoured undergraduates who had at least the semblance of intelligence (elsewhere, a title, inherited income or a friend in a high place was the sure passport to a place and preferment). Several of Arnold's Rugbeians already shone there, and the brilliance of Clough's entrance examination papers had created quite a stir among the Fellows. Yet almost from the moment he arrived, something went wrong. What, and why?

First, one must understand the narrowness and inefficiency of the educational system which Oxford offered. The curriculum was confined to theology, classics and a little mathematics or logic: coming as he did from Rugby, where a spirit of wide-ranging intellectual curiosity open to the realities of the modern world prevailed, Clough found little in the Oxford system to stimulate him. By today's standards, the colleges were tiny. Few of them housed more than a dozen Fellows and 40 undergraduates (only a minority of whom aspired to an honours degree). The principal medium of teaching was the lecture, delivered on stock subjects to classes of about 20: if you wanted individual attention, you had to find someone willing to coach you and pay him by the hour. Otherwise, apart from writing essays and sitting exams, students were very much left to themselves. Women formed no part of the university, and only those prepared to subscribe to the Church of England were admitted. Compared with German equivalents, the standard of scholarship was abysmally low.

Not surprisingly, these constraints made Oxford a stifling and atrophied environment. Against the force of smug and lazy inertia, young men sought to open its gates and horizons: the Church of England was the focus of rebellion. In brief, three factions battled it out. Some took a fiercely Evangelical position, preaching a Bible-bashing Protestant fundamentalism which asked no sophisticated questions of religion and put a straitjacket on life. Others, influenced by the research of German scholars into the historical facts behind the story of Jesus, took a more liberal line. Like Dr Arnold, they thought that Anglicanism needed to drop most of its ritual and mythology, reconcile itself to Nonconformist sects and move with the times. The crucial figure here was one Dr

Renn Hampden, who in 1836 was proposed by the Prime Minister, Lord Melbourne, as Professor of Divinity. But Hampden angered conservatives by advocating that subscription to the 39 Articles, drawn up in the 16th-century as the basic framework of Anglican belief, should no longer be a condition of entry to the university, and his appointment was rejected by the governing body. Dr Arnold was enraged by this decision and in Hampden's defence published a fiery polemic in the *Edinburgh Review* entitled 'The Oxford Malignants'.

This was aimed specifically at yet another party of opposition to the status quo, the Tractarians, so-called after a series of tracts or essays that they periodically issued on points of doctrine. Their view was that the Church of England had lost its sense of spiritual direction and should return to its roots in the more mystical church of the Early Christian Fathers. Attempts to rationalise Christianity in accordance with scientific or historical practice were misguided: God was beyond the reach of human understanding, and the truth of the Christian religion could only be apprehended through ritual and sacrament. These positions seemed to bring the Tractarians and their allies the Puseyites (so-called after their leader Dr Pusey) close to Roman Catholicism and submission to the authority of the Pope – factors which associated them in certain quarters with the cause of reaction and made them politically suspect.

The most charismatic figure among the Tractarians was John Henry Newman, Fellow of Oriel College. Radiating seraphic calm, reluctant to get down and dirty in argument, Newman appeared so entirely and self-lessly devoted to higher things that his opponents found it hard to assail him. His sermons were wonders of gentle rhetoric and exhortation which seemed to cut effort-lessly through the thickets of doubt and dissension, and many of Clough's generation were mesmerised by their calmly articulated certainties. Decades later, Arnold's son Matthew would recall 'the charm of that spiritual appari-tion, gliding in the dim afternoon light through the aisles... rising into the pulpit, and then, in the most entrancing of voices, breaking the silence with words and thought which were a religious music – subtle, sweet, mournful', and wonder who could ever resist its allure.

But Newman was no charlatan of fine words and hot air. His intellect was diamond-sharp; he did not miss a trick. In response to 'The Oxford Malignants', he asked just one spot-on question, 'Is Dr Arnold a Christian?', which precisely encapsulated what was at stake. Somewhere a line had to be drawn: either God had revealed the truth through the Bible and the Church, or he had not; the liberals were mistaken in thinking they could select personal portfolios of belief, rejecting bits and pieces which did not convince them. Newman's clarity on this point was reassuring. 'One knows the worst of where the Tractarians are going,' wrote another Rugbeian at Oxford, Thomas Hughes. 'They may go to Rome, and there's an end of it. But the Germanisers are going to the abysses or no one knows where.'

One Oxford Fellow drawn to Tractarianism was a brilliant 25-year-old of manic-depressive tendencies called William George Ward. Possessed of both an enormous waistline and a rare logical tenacity, he was sometimes described as a combination of Falstaff and Socrates. The son of a Tory MP, educated at Winchester, he lectured in mathematics at Balliol. Religion obsessed him – more, one feels, as an intellectual challenge than as a spiritual need, and at the time of Clough's arrival in Oxford he was in the process of transferring his allegiance from the Broad Church to the Newmanite persuasion.

But Ward was also tremendously good fun. Shaggy and shabby in dress, fruity of voice, he was prone to extravagant superlatives ('detestable' and 'transcendental' being two of his favourite adjectives), and from his earliest years an artless candour earned him notoriety (at a children's party, he was once found in the corner sullenly biting his nails; asked by the hostess what the matter was, he replied, 'I expected to find it a bore, but now that I am here I find it even worse than I thought.') Today, he would be considered preposterously camp. Infatuated by everything to do with the theatre, he 'knew the names not only of the principal actors but of the supernumeraries and would note with interest how Mr Smith or Mr Jones who played First Footman or Policeman had gone from Haymarket to Covent Garden'. In the evenings, the floor of his rooms in Balliol would thunder and creak as he presented his friends with riotous solo performances of ballets he had invented, usually based 'on some event of university interest' like 'Mr Macmullen's dispute with the Regius Professor' and featuring elaborate pirouettes and entrechats.

So much for Ward's manic aspect; the depressiveness manifested itself in long periods of total inertia and violent migraine, as well as a desperate craving for affection. On young Clough, of the thick brown hair and sweetly earnest expression, his longings fixated with an intensity that neither of them would ever quite understand. In the all-male seminary that the university effectively was, theirs would be an unrequited love affair, which ended in a parting, if not a rift – a fascinating little episode in the history of Victorian emotionalism.

Clough had made a bad start at Oxford, from which he never altogether recovered. The problem was complex. Expectations of him were so high that he became frightened and confused. It was clear that people were waiting for him 'to come forward… and be a great personage, and develop my views & be the leader of a great party of disciples'. But were such ambitions spiritually legitimate? Or had he crossed the thin line into mere worldly egotism? In his diary, he sarcastically flagellates himself: 'I am marvellously well pleased with my wretched attainments and enjoy above all playing with God's word to feed my vanity. May he forgive me and show me my great wickedness.'

On top of this came Ward's irresistible attentions, which threw him into a flat spin. Ward was deserting the Broad Church and could not leave his beloved behind. He took Clough off to hear Newman's Tractarian sermons and bludgeoned him afterwards. With unremitting, unanswerable logic, he explained to Clough why his Arnoldian views were wrong and told him what he should be doing and thinking and believing. 'I have found out from Ward the chief source of my difficulties & perplexities, viz. a false idea, presumptuous & rationalistic, that what we are to do here is to make ourselves holy, supposing that we can acquire qualities making us fit for Heaven, & that to acquire such is our grand object, whereas it is really to do God's will to love (i) him and (ii) our neighbour,' he writes wanly in his diary.

Finally, however, he gave up. Ward's logic may have been unassailable, but for Clough it missed the point. He did not want to be flung against the ropes and forced into the Newmanite corner; Ward was demanding more than he could give. 'His lack of poetical perceptions & of quietness destroy much of the sympathies of daily inter-course,' Clough complained. If only he could stick to 'pleasant small talk' and not 'talk about theological matters & so continually'. 'I feel like a bit of paper blown up the chimney by a draught,' he wrote to a Rugby friend, 'and one doesn't always feel like being a piece of paper.' It was a plaint that would resound through the rest of his life.

Clough was also dimly aware that Ward's importuning went beyond the bounds of ordinary friendship. Even though one can doubt that anything which we would describe as sexual contact occurred, there were moments when Ward's attentions became 'indelicate', as when he begged Clough to call him 'dear' and asked him 'to make unnatural demonstrations'. Clough hardly knew how to deal with such overtures, and seems to have handled the situation by evasion rather than confrontation. The relationship dragged on, to the discomfort of them both: Clough drifted into spending more time with old Rugby friends like the aspiring poet Thomas Burbidge, and Ward wrote him the long, jealous, wounding, self-justifying letters of a lover who knows he is losing the game.

This was the shadow which loured over Clough's

undergraduate years and stopped him being the person he wanted to be. It wasn't all misery: he enjoyed 'skiffing' and bathing on the river, and was admitted to an elite debating club, The Decade. But the diaries make it plain that he wasn't happy. When Ward left him alone, which was not often, a rather more feeble character called William Tylden took his place, following Clough with a dog-like devotion that proved as irritating as Ward's overweening possessiveness.

Social life in college otherwise revolved around bois-terous 'wine parties', held at all times of the day and night. Clough hated the way that they encouraged him to drink too much and show off. Life became unsatisfactory, unsatisfying. He fell prey to periods of mooching indo-lence during which he lazed around in bed and wasted time reading novels by the sensational new author of the day, Charles Dickens. His concentration began to falter and his academic performance slipped – a trail of anxious psychosomatic symptoms developed in tandem. Perhaps because the subject was taught by Ward, he found the mathematical side of the Oxford honours course hard to grasp, and even his entry for the university's English verse prize – on the subject of Salsette and Elephanta, islands off the Indian coast, famous for their temple caves – was trumped by a Christ Church man called John Ruskin. Significantly, Clough's stiffly Miltonic ode took as its theme the notion that the caves represent the fount of all religions – a 'primeval Truth divine' – of which Christianity was only one off-shoot, no more or less valid than Buddhism or Hinduism. Far from moving closer to the heart of the Church, as Ward wanted, he was toying (thanks in part to his reading of the radical German theologians) with the dangerous idea of abandoning it altogether.

Clough's family had now returned to Liverpool. In 1839 he spoke to his father about the matter of the asterisks and the next day consulted the family doctor: the diary records no more detail of the discussions, which appear to have made no difference. His solace was the countryside, and in vacations he hiked with friends through both Wordsworth's Lake District (often staying with the Arnolds at their holiday home) and Scotland. Both the landscape and the people who inhabited it revitalised him: once in the Highlands he encountered a poor crofter with a sick child and was so concerned that he walked two days to Fort William and then back again in order to bring the child some medicine.

His diary also records long daily walks around Oxford, most of them solitary. There is something mysterious about the routes he took, and faint hints are recorded of some motivation other than exercise. What, for example, is implied by the entry for 5 May 1841: 'Woodeaton and *ta susanika*'? '*Ta susanika*' is the Greek for 'the Susan thing'. But who was Susan? The editor of the diaries, Anthony Kenny, researched local parish birth records and discovered the existence of a Susanna Neale, a 16-year-old shoemaker's daughter.

There was another class of woman, however, which wouldn't have featured in such records: Oxford was notoriously rife with prostitutes, attracted to the city by the prospect of rich pickings among the undergraduates. Estimates of their numbers vary between 400 and 800. An anonymous essay entitled 'Public Morals: Prostitution in Oxford', published in the *Oxford Protestant Magazine* in 1847, asserts 'that their number is large there can be no doubt. Our streets bear their open & painful testimony. The pleasant walks, the shady lanes, the straggling cottages of surrounding hamlets, testify their multitude. So soon as the shades of evening descend, many are the streets and passages which cannot be travelled by the modest and uncontaminated youth, without both eye and ear being assailed by scenes and language too gross to mention.'

The university proctors were empowered to police the problem by arresting suspects who strayed near the colleges. As the writer quoted above indicates, many of them evaded this danger by positioning themselves on the roads outside the city's centre. The surviving lists of those arrested show that while many of them came on a seasonal basis from London, many more lived in the surrounding villages such as Woodeaton to which Clough persistently walked in the evenings. It is inconceivable that he would not have seen them, and, as one turns the sad pages of the proctors' registers, it is impossible not to speculate whether *ta susanika* might refer to Susan Longford, Susan Collinson, Susan Parker, Susan Bevan, Susan Stephens, Susannah Slater, Susannah Hilliard, Susannah Colgrave or Susannah Nobbs, all of whom are listed there. Further than this we cannot go.

In 1841 Clough's fourth and last year as an undergraduate, his self-pity plumbed new depths. 'My present state, I fear, must be very bad,' he writes. 'I feel myself to be feeding on all sorts of garbage.' His friends joked that he deliberately kept his rooms freezing cold in order to discourage visitors and wine parties. He started to work feverishly hard, but to no avail: in his final exams, as he told his sister Annie, he 'did the papers much worse than I expected' and was duly placed in the undistinguished Second Class. The rest of Oxford was amazed; despite all his troubles and diffidence he had kept his reputation as a Balliol Scholar of outstanding intellectual brilliance, and such a performance, adequate in anyone else's case, for him seemed like a disaster and a disgrace. As an older Oxford Rugbeian, Arthur Stanley, later Dean of Westminster and Arnold's biographer, wrote to another of Clough's friends: 'I maintain that he is the profoundest man of his years that ever I saw, or that Rugby ever sent forth... [but] academically speaking, who was ever so unfortunate – so able, so laborious, and yet so unaccountably failing?'

Clough was on a hike from Oxford to Rugby when the result came to him, and he made a brave show of not minding the humiliation. To Annie he wrote, 'You must really not trouble yourself about my class. I do not care a straw for it myself... I suppose a good many whom I ought to wish to gratify are disappointed a good deal... otherwise it does not matter I think at all; and I can assure you it has not lessened my own opinion of my ability – for I did my papers not a quarter as well as my reading would naturally have enabled me to do and if I got a 2nd with my little finger it would not have taken two hands to get a double first.' Yet even at a purely material level, the result was worrying: his father's cotton trading was doing badly, and Clough could not count on him for financial support. The lack of a First Class degree to his name would not help his employment prospects.

He told Arnold the news in person – to what reaction we do not know, although Arnold's son Tom remembered Clough standing in the middle of Rugby School courtyard and saying, 'with face partly flushed and partly pale...

"I have failed".' But perhaps Oxford failed Clough, rather than vice versa. 'I had been pretty well sated of distinctions and competitions at school,' he reported to a commission on the future of the Oxford syllabus in 1852. 'I would gladly have dispensed with anything more of success in this kind... What I wanted was to sit down to happy, unimpeded prosecution of some new subject or subjects; surely there was more in the domain of knowledge than that Latin and Greek which I had been wandering about in for the last ten years... An infinite lassitude and impatience, which I saw reflected in the faces of others, quickly began to infect me.' In Oxford today, among those who have achieved highly in the nurturing environment of a public school, this remains a familiar *cri de coeur*.

He spent the rest of the summer of 1841 walking, writing a few poems and coaching university candidates. 'Nice boys, and I liked the work; boy-teaching is far preferable to man-teaching,' he wrote. 'It was also very profitable, most of my Papas being rich.' This sort of teaching continued to bring him both income and pleasure, and with at least one of his charges he seems to have fallen romantically in love. Theodore Walrond was another head boy at Rugby, who won, under Clough's tutelage, a scholarship to Balliol. He was a gloriously handsome lad, a superb athlete and an accomplished classical scholar. Clough was bewitched by another version of himself. 'Possessed wholly by Walrond', he wrote gnomically in his diary, repeatedly scrawling his name in Greek script all over the cover. Fortunately, the relationship resolved itself into firm friendship, but not before Clough had plunged into savage gloom – a delayed reaction to his exam failure, perhaps.

After Walrond, he conceived another infatuation for a teenage boy, one Thomas Battersby. His health slumped. He suffered from 'night-time visions' and contemplated taking confession at one point, so great was his self-disgust. 'I seem to know nothing except that I am wholly wrong within,' he wrote in his diary, complaining in the next sentence of 'the filthiness and falseness of my imagination', and rebuking himself for 'continual takings of help & love & then cutting them'. On the blow of Dr Arnold's sudden and premature death from a heart attack in June 1842 ('Thank God for having sent me this pain. I never had pain before, and I feel it is good for me. I am so thankful,' were reported to be among his last earthly words), Clough makes no recorded comment at all.

But then things got better. Although he lost out on a Fellowship at Balliol, Clough did win a Fellowship at another leading Oxford college, Oriel, where his 17 common-room colleagues included John Henry Newman and several other prominent Tractarians and Romish sympathisers. It was a materially comfortable posting, offering plenty of time for the reading and walking and chatting which were Clough's meat and drink, but it came at a price. In order to become a Fellow of an Oxford or Cambridge college, one had to possess an MA degree, and, in order to be awarded an MA degree, one was required to subscribe one's name to the 39 Articles of the Church of England. For all but the most scrupulous or conscientious, this was not actually very difficult: the Articles carefully avoid controversy or superstition and allow for broad interpretation. They specify, for instance, belief in original sin and the resurrection, but not in the existence of purgatory or the infallibility of the Church. One might compare the level of hypocrisy involved in nodding assent to that of a republican standing up for 'God Save the Queen'.

So Clough shut his eyes and signed. However, he was not at all happy about the gesture: it ranked for him, after all, as the cardinal sin of his era, hypocrisy. 'It is not so much from any objection to this or that point as general dislike to [sic] subscription and strong feeling of its being after all… a bondage, and a very heavy one, and one that may cramp one and cripple one for life,' he wrote to his Rugbeian friend John Gell in Tasmania. A year later, he wrote to Gell again, and his attitude to the problem had if anything hardened: 'If I begin to think about God, there [arise] a thousand questions, and whether the 39 Articles answer them at all or whether I should not answer them in the most diametrically opposite purport is a matter of great doubt. If I am to study the questions, I have no right to put my name to the answers beforehand... ' What he meant but did not quite say was that far from following Newman and Ward on the high road to Rome, he was more inclined to overtake the late Dr Arnold on the path to Germany and make for the school of liberal criticism, where the very foundations of religion were being explored and undermined. Clough could no longer be sure he was a Christian, and in the 1840s that was a very dizzying precipice to be peering over.

So much so that he retreated from the edge. There was life to be lived and, once he had settled down at Oriel, he managed the young man's trick of shelving long-term problems and enjoying himself instead. Clough's first years at Oriel were his golden days: it was as though he had suddenly discovered confidence and come into focus. The strenuously earnest schoolboy who became the anxious, shoe-gazing undergraduate now blossomed into a convivial, high-spirited, funny and energetic young don, and those who knew him at this time always felt that they had caught the best of him. At the centre of his social circle were two sons of Dr Arnold – the elegantly Frenchified Matthew (who teased Clough by addressing him as 'my love') and generous-hearted, straight-down-the-line Tom. Together with the exemplary Theodore Walrond, they idled and smoked, ate huge breakfasts and drank too much, joshed each other, giggled about women, skiffed on the Cherwell and walked on the hills – over 20 years later, in his poem 'Thyrsis', Matthew Arnold would nostalgically turn his memories of these days into the stuff of a classical idyll.

They were serious, too, or at least radical in their politics. This was a period during which revolution burgeoned all over Europe – the 1840s could be compared to the 1960s, as a decade when young men's hopes were untarnished by bitter experience. At Oxford, Clough and his friends turned republicans and reformers, speaking out against the privileges of aristocracy, the degradations of industrialism and the cynicism of *laissez-faire* capitalism – such views were the logical extension of their Rugbeian education. A great influence on them all was the Scots philosopher Thomas Carlyle, with his vision of a new form of religion, purged of superstition and sectarianism but rich in spiritual exaltation drawn from nature, and his insistence that only hard, honest work could redeem society from its present decadence. Clough took Carlyle's injunctions to heart, and realised that for someone in his cushioned position bleeding hearts and speechifying were not enough. So for several years he worked regular shifts at a shelter in the slums of St Ebbe's run by the Oxford Mendicity Society, a charity which ministered to deserving beggars, giving them a roof for the night and tickets which they could exchange for food and lodging. It wasn't something he talked about much.

The question of women also preoccupied him. Despite his knowledge that the university statutes made it almost impossible for a college Fellow to marry, he showed great interest in them, at several levels. His solitary walks round Oxford continued. In 1845 he was thrilled and scandalised at the public display of naked flesh offered by the celebrated *sylphide* ballerina Marie Taglioni and threw her a bouquet. He was much taken with Walrond's graceful and quick-witted sister Agnes, and even wrote to Annie of 'her whom I hope someday to see your sister' – but Agnes proved 'very slow to advance' and ended up marrying an MP. Maybe this was the disappointment that he stoically commemorated in some stray lines of poetry:

> Quiet, my sweet one, my heart
> Though it may crack, it won't break

Other writing of this period reveals a more frustrated and tormented aspect to his sexuality. 'Adam and Eve' is an incomplete poetic drama which opens with Adam's mortified guilt at a sin symbolised by the eating of the forbidden apple:

Since that last evening we have fallen indeed
Yes we have fallen my Eve Oh yes –
One, two, and three, and four – the appetite
The enjoyment, the aftervoid, the thinking of it
Specially the latter two, most specially the last.

Another fragment is charged with nightmarish imagery of masturbation and castration:

Should not the holy and preventive hand
With one short act, decisive for all time
By sharp excism pluck the unsprouted seed
Sever the seed of ill
There are the scripture tells us who have done it [sic].

Out of all this fear and panic came one beautiful and distinctive poem – 'Natura Naturans' ('Creating Nature'). The Poet sits beside an unknown girl in a railway carriage, and picks up that faint but unmistakable bat-squeak sensation:

She spake not, no, nor looked at me:
From her to me, from me to her
What passed so subtly, stealthily?

This is, of course, the sexual instinct – the electricity of desire which courses through the world and motivates propagation. The phenomenon was much discussed by the pre-Darwinian biologists of the time: birds do it, bees do it, living things from 'lichen small on granite wall' to 'the leopard lithe in Indian glade' do it. The poem is sometimes obscure in its syntax, but it is also witty and lyrical, and its theme is clear: the poet wants to couple with the girl, the girl wants to couple with him:

> We sat while o'er and in us, more
> And more, a power unknown prevailed
> Inhaling and inhaled – and still
> 'Twas one, inhaling and inhaled.

Morality has nothing to do with it. In the mid 1840s, this was a shocking notion: sexual longing and pleasure were male prerogatives, of which women were supposed to be merely the passive recipient, and the presence of the sanctifying term 'love' was the only way to justify them. But love doesn't interest Clough here; this is a poem about an itch and the urge to scratch it.

Behind the sly ebullience of 'Natura Naturans' lies Clough's discovery of George Sand, the French novelist who made sense of the whole sex problem. Sand's fiction was the favourite secret reading of the freer spirits among the 1840s generation, and literary history still underrates the sensational impact she had in England – Charlotte and Emily Brontë, for instance, would not be the same writers without it. Nowadays she is generally remembered as a cigar-smoking, trouser-wearing, Chopin-loving proponent of free love, but for Clough and his friends she was a nobler thing by far – 'a Socrates among the sophists', Clough called her – embodying a broader philosophy of liberation, in which the personal was intertwined with the political, and Rousseauan sincerity and candour of emotion transcended all class barriers and social conventions. In her novels, a duke can marry a peasant and a wife can leave her husband for another man. Women, as much as men, have a right to their desires. A loveless marriage is no marriage, and the stigma society attaches to seduction, elopement and adultery is meaningless if genuine feeling validates it. Conventional manners must be discounted, whatever the resulting scandal. Love acts in the name of a higher, purer law, and the only sin is to deny it.

The honesty to one's self promulgated by George Sand became increasingly important to Clough, and, behind all the schoolboyish gaiety of his Oxford life, he was seeking a way out of the compromise with the 39 Articles that his Fellowship at Oriel represented. He pondered emigration and investigated the possibility of posts at institutions like the newly established University of London, which posed no such religious tests on its teaching staff. In England, few other callings were open to him: he had no money (his father had died impoverished, leaving him with financial responsibilities for his mother and sister), he had no bent for the law, and he was not the sort of person who could easily sue for patrons in high places. Poetry he regarded as little more than a hobby: he didn't have the ego or the missionary enthusiasm to write with professional determination, and, even if he had been fired to do so, it would have been impossible to make a living from his pen without recourse to journalism or the novel. Oddly, he seems never to have considered the soft option chosen by many of his friends in a similar position: schoolmastering at Rugby. He liked teaching, he liked boys – one can only assume that the shadow of Dr Arnold cast some sort of chill on his soul.

Meanwhile, religious controversy was rocking the old order at Oxford – attacked from two fronts, the tyranny of the 39 Articles began to crumble. In 1844, Clough's old Balliol friend WG Ward, of whom he now saw little, had published *The Idea of a Christian Church*. By announcing in its pages that subscription to the Articles was perfectly compatible with the doctrines of Catholicism, Ward implied that Anglicanism was schismatic, if not pointless. This was one step too far for the university's authorities, who proceeded formally to condemn the book and to strip Ward of his degrees. Ward responded by resigning his Fellowship, converting to Rome and – much to everybody's astonished amusement – taking himself a wife, with whom he proceeded to father a large brood of children.

Shortly after this fracas, a more convincing spiritual guide, John Henry Newman, was also received into the Roman Catholic Church. Then, in 1846, there appeared an English translation (the work of a young woman, living in Coventry, later to be famous as George Eliot) of the German theologian David Strauss's biography of Jesus. Basing its arguments on new archaeological and textual scholarship, it interpreted Christ's birth, miracles and resurrection as myth, put his life and teaching into a firmly historical context, and opened up the way to outright atheism. The battlelines were now firmly drawn.

Clough preferred to stay well out of the crossfire. His personal beliefs were closer to Strauss's than they were to Ward's or Newman's, but he wished them to remain only that – personal. He stood up for Ward's right to say what he felt, but in the name of what he called 'the vital atmosphere of truth' deplored 'the stifling gas of men's opinion'. He was repelled by the hypocrisy of so many Christians – their say-one-thing and do-another mentality, their readiness to tip their hats and pay their sixpenny due before returning to a life of lying, cheating and exploitation. Inverting a remark of Dr Arnold's to the effect that the 19th century needed a new set of Commandments, Clough wrote his own almost blasphemously satirical version. 'The Latest Decalogue' is couched in the casual rhyming doggerel of the airy man-about-town, and like Swift's pamphlet suggesting the merits of cannibalism 'A Modest Proposal', its effect is all the stronger for its plausibly straight face:

Honour thy parents, that is, all
From whom advancement may fall:
Thou shalt not kill; but needst not strive
Officiously to keep alive;
Do not adultery commit
Advantage rarely comes of it:
Thou shalt not steal; an empty feat
When it's so lucrative to cheat.

And he asked, as have many since, how a Christ would fare if he returned to human existence today. Not very well, he supposes, as he imagines Jesus sitting disconsolately by his own grave:

And the great world, it chanced, came by that way,
And stopped and looked, and spoke to the police,
And said the thing, for order's sake and peace
Must certainly be suppressed, the nuisance cease.

So why bother with Christianity at all? To us, this seems an obvious question: 150 years ago, it implied a leap into the outer darkness, and Clough was hesitant about asking it. He began reading about other religions, especially Buddhism. 'I cannot feel sure that a man may not have all that is important in Christianity even if he does not so much as know that Jesus of Nazareth existed,' he wrote in a letter to Annie in 1847, and that is about as far as he would venture. If others wanted to fall down and worship, let them do so, but, for himself, he felt he couldn't worship what he didn't understand. Nor could he continue to tolerate the endless circular controversies, the theological nit-picking, the vicious High Table arguments, the factions and sects and defections and conversions: there were more important things to worry about. In this he was at one with others in his Oxford generation – young Tom Arnold, for instance, who escaped the issue of the 39 Articles by emigrating to the empty colony of New Zealand. There he hoped to contribute to a new model of human society, free of hierarchy and repression, mendicity and mendacity – a George Sand society. 'Let us work at things which we know,' he wrote back to England. 'Let us shorten the hours of labour for the poor; let us purify our cities; let us unfetter our trade – surely we can unite for these objects. As for religion we must agree to differ.' (Alas, the New Zealand experiment did not work. Tom Arnold returned to England and in 1856 converted to Catholicism.)

At the beginning of 1848, Clough announced his intention of resigning from his tutorial position at Oriel. To proceed any further with his academic career, he would need to take Holy Orders in the Church of England, renounce the possibility of marriage and subscribe yet again to the 39 Articles. This, in all conscience, he could not do, as he informed Edward Hawkins, the college's kindly Provost, who made every effort to persuade him to bide his time. But Clough was adamant that he could only offer 'the ordinary negative acquiescence of a layman', and there for a while the situation rested.

At this crucial moment, Clough encountered the American philosopher Ralph Waldo Emerson, who was visiting England on a lecture tour. A friend of Carlyle, he had heard about Clough on the grapevine and invited himself to stay in Oxford. Emerson knew something of what Clough was going through; he had resigned from his position as a Unitarian minister, and now preached another sort of gospel which neither denied nor asserted the claims of Christianity, emphasising instead the paramount importance of the individual self following its own inner light, inspired by nature rather than a body of written doctrine. This was what Clough wanted to hear, and it heartened him. Emerson's thought moved freely and easily, untrammelled by the complexities of English prejudices and traditions. It didn't bully or hector, it wasn't knotted with anxiety, and Emerson wanted nothing from him except intelligent conversation. '[He] wholly declines *roaring*... There is no dogmatism or arbitrariness or positiveness about him,' Clough wrote to Tom Arnold – and in warring Oxford that quietness was a tonic. At Emerson's suggestion, they slipped over to Paris to see for themselves the effects of the revolution which two months previously had overthrown the monarchy and set up a republic. Clough was too much of a sceptic to become any sort of political activist, but he was sympathetic to many of the socialists' goals and hopeful of political progress. Together with Emerson, he spent four happy weeks in the French capital, visiting the sights and listening to the great orators of the day. Their respective journals contain entries which suggest that they also had some serious talk about a subject which preoccupied Clough – namely sex, and specifically prostitution, the prevalence of which in English cities had appalled the pure-minded Emerson from clean-living New England, and which doubtless shocked him in Paris too. Don't be a fool, Dickens had snorted when he raised the subject at a dinner party, 'chastity in the male sex was as good as gone in our own times', and if his own son were particularly chaste 'he should be alarmed on his account as if he could not be in good health.'

By the end of the trip, Emerson and Clough had become fast friends and, in tribute to Clough's open-mindedness, Emerson reported to New England that he 'had found in London, the best American'. Back home,

Clough attended a course of Emerson's lectures and then went to Liverpool to bid him farewell. As the ship was about to set sail, so the story goes, Clough asked, 'What shall we do without you? Think where we are. Carlyle has led us all out into the wilderness and he has left us there.' 'That is what all the young men in England have said to me,' Emerson replied, laying a jokily benedictory hand on Clough's head. 'I ordain you Bishop of England to go up and down among all the young men and lead them into the promised land.'

But Bishop of England was exactly what Clough did not wish to be: he simply longed to be left alone, to believe what he chose to believe, in the privacy of his own mind, and over the rest of the summer his determination to resign altogether from Oriel and Oxford was consolidated. 'I do not feel my position is tenable in any way,' he finally wrote – with uncharacteristic firmness – to Provost Hawkins in October. 'I can have nothing whatever to do with a subscription to the XXXIX Articles – and deeply repent of having ever submitted to one.' How he might shape his future he did not quite know. A letter to Tom Arnold shows him keen to idle and travel for a time. He did not rule out the idea of following Tom to New Zealand. But, meanwhile, he claimed to be 'extremely jolly... rejoicing in my emancipation' and living 'in the daily possibility of falling in love'. There was no hurry: he had a bit of teaching, and was 'doing the literary a little'.

That little was in fact rather large. The glorious monument to these months of liberation is Clough's first major poem, 'The Bothie of Tober-na-Vuolich'. Amounting to about 1,700 lines, it is divided into nine books, after the model of the classical epic. And like the *Iliad* and the *Aeneid*, it is written in hexameters – which is to say, each line divides into six metric feet, containing two or three more syllables than the pentameter of Shakespeare, Milton and Wordsworth. Because of its lack of rhythmic fluency and grace, hexameter has rarely been used in English verse, although Clough was inspired to adopt it after reading another long narrative poem, the lachrymose *Evangeline*, by the American Longfellow, published in 1847. As the quotations below will demonstrate, the effect of hexameter is flat and blunt, heavier in stress, crisper in consonants and more rumbustious than that of the airier pentameter. But its piston rhythm makes it good for storytelling, good for jokes, good for surprises – and Clough exploits these qualities to the hilt.

Subtitled 'a long-vacation pastoral', 'The Bothie' (a highland cottage) opens with a group of Oxford undergraduates spending part of the summer in Scotland on a reading party. To this extent Clough draws directly on his own experience: together with Tom Arnold, Walrond and others, he enjoyed several such holidays, laconically recorded in his diary with entries such as 'The deer drive. Adolphus and his men. Long John. John McDonald, Duncan Cameron etc. etc. McKeen, the feast and the carouse. The song & the dance, even unto 5am.'

'The Bothie' delights in all the colour and comedy of the Highlands, celebrating the hardy, unspoilt ways of its inhabitants and the rugged glory of the landscape. But it moves on: the heart of the poem is the journey taken by the awkward, independent radical Philip Hewson – a self-portrait of the poet, one guesses, with elements of Tom Arnold as well. In Book III, he leaves the camaraderie of his Oxford friends to hike alone through the glens:

> Weary of reading am I, and weary of walks prescribed us;
> Weary of Ethic and Logic, of Rhetoric yet more weary,
> Eager to range over heather unfettered of gillie and marquis,
> I will away with the rest, and bury my dismal classics.

On his little odyssey, in the eponymous bothie, he finds true love in the shape of the farmer's daughter Elspie Mackaye, one of the most self-assured and unsimpering of Victorian heroines. Educated by her father 'to help myself and others', she works in the fields and reads voraciously at night. The result is that she has an entirely unprejudiced view of the world, and will not let Philip patronise her:

> What, she said, and if I have let you become my sweetheart,

I am to read no books! But you may go your ways then,
And I will read, she said, with my father at home as I used to.
If you must have it, he said, I myself will read them to you.
Well, she said, but no, I will read to myself when I choose it...

After one of the most fresh and touching courtships in English literature, they marry and emigrate to New Zealand.

One modern critic has called 'The Bothie' 'a revolutionary poem about love', and indeed it is that, with George Sand as its inspiration. Clough had wanted to translate her novel *Jeanne*, but felt that his French wasn't up to it. Instead he wrote 'The Bothie' – a tribute to her spirit and, more specifically, to *Jeanne*, the tale of a dashing English milord with socialist views who visits the country with his chums for some hunting and there meets a French peasant girl whom he marries. But 'The Bothie' is not just about love. It is also bursting with the sort of instinctive sexual desire which permeates 'Natura Naturans'. Boys look longingly at the flesh of girls:

In a blue cotton print tucked up over striped linsey-woolsey,
Barefoot, barelegged, he beheld her, with arms bare up to the
elbows,
Bending with fork in her hand in a garden uprooting potatoes.

And girls have their fantasies, too. Women in Clough's

poetry, incidentally, are never the submissive victims, silent muses, or vessels of purity that one repeatedly encounters among his contemporaries (Tennyson's Maud, Matthew Arnold's Marguerite, Coventry Patmore's Angel in the House). On the contrary, like the novelistic heroines of Trollope or George Eliot, they are audible, visible and articulate presences with wills of their own. Elspie even has her own libido, albeit unconsciously. 'Sometimes', she explains, with pre-Freudian ingenuousness, she dreams of herself as a bridge being built, and

> ... of a great invisible hand coming down, and
> Dropping the great key-stone in the middle: there in my
>> dreaming,
> There I feel the great key-stone coming in, and through it
> Feel the other part – all the other stones of the archway,
> Joined into mine with a strange happy sense of completeness.

On the title-page of the first edition of 'The Bothie', Clough warns the reader 'to expect every kind of irregularity in these modern hexameters'. It is that sort of poem, with a wonderful devil-may-care spontaneity about it. A modesty, too; it has no pretensions to taking on the masters at their own game, to out-Wordsworth Wordsworth or to out-soar Shelley. Clough had no sense of self-importance as a poet, and not much ambition. One feels that he wrote for his own pleasure, when the spirit moved him, and, although his manuscripts show him to have been a furious crosser-out and reviser, he was not one to agonise over *le mot juste* or hone the exquisitely musical Tennysonian cadence. Close textual analysis of his verbal intricacies would not take a reader very far; the poem's parade of mock-epic similes, inversions, repetitions, invocations and tag phrases are more playful than poetically skilful. Technically speaking, his edges are rough and bear even less scrutiny: in his efforts to communicate a complex chain of thought, he often stumbles into a metrical or grammatical muddle. For all that, 'The Bothie' remains a marvel. In composition it gushed forth at headlong speed, and one feels that Clough did not pause to channel the flow, let alone blot the line: charged with the optimism and idealism of 1848, it is a young man's work, and its rip-roaring, tireless energy makes it the most youthfully exuberant of the great Victorian poems.

'The Bothie' enjoyed widespread and immediate success. The *Saturday Review*'s critique praised it as 'full of fun, of jokes bad and good, of discussions, of adventure, of love-making, of deep feeling'. Elizabeth Barrett Browning thought it 'full of vigour and freshness, & with passages & indeed whole scenes of great beauty & eloquence'. 'Tennyson must look to his laurels,' added a delighted Emerson, who passed his copy round Boston society. Among its few detractors was Matthew Arnold, himself a writer of verse more classically correct and conventionally elevating: on the one hand, he liked the 'sincerity' of 'The Bothie' and its attempt 'to get breast to breast with reality'; on the other, he felt it suffered from 'a deficiency of the sense of the beautiful'. With the languid candour which his friends learnt to expect of him, he wrote to Clough, 'I doubt your being an *artist*' – and he was probably right to do so.

A small embarrassment relates to the title. A Gaelic speaker pointed out that its original title, 'Toper-na-Fuosich', was slang for the female genitalia (literally, 'the bearded well'). Clough was amused but, in deference to the decencies, changed the offending words, and this wonderful poem was from then on known as 'The Bothie of Tober-na-Vuolich' – a name which means absolutely nothing at all.

After leaving Oriel, Clough returned to Liverpool and spent a couple of months living with his mother and sister. The enthusiastic reception granted 'The Bothie' had stimulated him to decision. Early in 1849, in partnership with his (thoroughly mediocre) friend Thomas Burbidge, he published a volume of poems entitled *Ambarvalia*, gathering together the efforts of his Oxford years. He also found himself a proper job. From October, he would serve as Principal of University Hall, a small residence for students attending University College, London. Although set up by Unitarians (who deny the divinity of Christ and the Trinity, preferring to believe in a single Godhead), the college claimed to be non-sectarian, and the post, combining teaching and pastoral responsibilities, appeared to steer clear of all religious controversies and subscriptions.

Happier than he would ever be again, Clough now set off for a few months of holiday and adventure. In April, he landed up in Rome, where Mazzini had recently led another revolution and set up a republican government. Unfortunately, the French decided to rally to the Pope's cause and its huge, efficient army began to besiege the city. As a foreigner, Clough could have secured a *laissez-passer* had the situation become imminently dangerous but, for the time being, people went about their normal business and there was very little in the way of military action: 'I went up to the Pincian Hill and saw the smoke and heard the occasional big cannon and the sharp succession of skirmishers' volleys bang, bang, bang,' he related to Annie. The city's monuments and great sights did not much impress him – 'Rome in general might be called a rubbishy place,' he told his mother – but he relished the strange poignant comedy of the siege and felt it would be 'a bore to do all the necessary things for getting away'. So he stayed and watched. At times he was also moved by the hopeless heroism of the republicans – it is from this period that Churchill's favourite, 'Say Not the Struggle Naught

Availeth', dates. But by mid-July French firepower had prevailed over Roman virtue, and Clough was free to leave. He was ready to set off for Florence, but changed his mind and eventually travelled back to London via Naples, Genoa, Turin and Geneva.

This episode in Clough's life is scantily documented by his correspondence. In a letter to his mother, he mentions some 'acquaintance' who has moved on to Florence and whom he plans to follow. There is no further evidence to support the idea that he was involved in some sort of romantic tangle, but his next great poem, 'Amours de Voyage', like 'The Bothie', clearly has some roots in Clough's own experience. Divided into five cantos, it is told through a series of letters from Italy. Claude – the name suggests Clough himself – is an intellectually sophisticated but disaffected young Englishman, caught up in the muddle of the Roman republic. Writing to his friend Eustace in hexameters, he reflects wryly on the ramifications of the political situation and the undulations of his tenuous involvement with another English traveller, the charming Mary Trevellyn, whose letters to her friend Miss Roper appear in counterpoint.

Claude has the Oxford graduate's self-importance and snobbishness, but his real problem is that he can't commit, either to the revolution or to Mary. A quotation from a French novel (presumably one of George Sand's) stands as an epigraph to the poem – '*Il doutait de tout, même de l'amour*' ('He had doubts about everything, even about love') – and that existential uncertainty makes Claude a Victorian Hamlet. He is cursed with an ironic sensibility which leads him in circles round every choice and action. He could do something practical to help the republic, he could even join in the fighting, but he dreads being pushed into anything 'factitious' – his favourite word, the 19th-century equivalent of 'phoney'. He cannot believe in things just because it is convenient to do so. He has a vivid fear of possible consequences. Action, he concludes:

> Is a most dangerous thing; I tremble for something factitious,
> Some malpractice of heart and illegitimate process;
> We are so prone to these things with our terrible notions of
> duty.

But this leaves him sitting in cafés, numb and unable to connect. In one unforgettable image, he describes himself as being like someone lowered with a rope round his waist into a cave, hovering over life:

> … wheresoever I swing, whether to shore, or to shelf, or
> Floor of cavern untrodden, shell-sprinkled, enchanting, I
> know I
> Yet shall one time feel the strong cord tighten about me, –
>
> Feel it, relentless, upbear me from spots I would rest in.

What are his feelings for the charming Mary? He is not sure. 'I am in love, you say; I do not think so exactly,' he writes to Eustace. But, even if he was, would that be enough justification for

Tying I know not what ties, which, whatever they are, I know
one thing,
Will, and must, woe is me, be one day painfully broken?

'Hang this thinking, at last!' he cries. 'What good is it? Oh, and what evil.' Yet at the end of the poem – which has no real climax, but concludes with crossed lines and misunderstanding – only the knowledge that comes from thinking consoles and sustains him:

Faith, I think, does pass, and love; but Knowledge abideth.
Let us seek Knowledge – the rest must come and go as it
happens.
Knowledge is hard to seek, and harder yet to adhere to.
Knowledge is painful often; and yet when we know, we are
happy.
Seek it, and leave mere Faith and Love to come with the
chances.

In this mood of fatalism, Claude sails for Egypt, while Mary shrugs her shoulders at his peculiar behaviour and returns to England.

Professor John Goode has called 'Amours de Voyage'

'the major masterpiece of high Victorian poetry'. It is also extraordinarily original, if not unique. Clough was always reluctant to pontificate on matters literary, but one essay he wrote in 1852 indicates a belief that the poetry of his age had reached something of a dead end. To escape the dominating idiom and diction of post-Keatsian romanticism, with all its sentimentalising and mythologising, he proposed verse which dealt 'more than at present it usually does, with general wants, ordinary feelings, the obvious rather than the rare facts of human nature', verse which connected with contemporary realities and touched and held people in the way that novels like *Vanity Fair* and *Bleak House* did. (He would surely have admired TS Eliot's *The Waste Land*.)

Whether Clough actually succeeded in addressing 'ordinary' wants and feelings is questionable – Claude is a rarefied individual – but his poetry is certainly rooted in a sense of the here-and-now. Nor is there any goo or slush or cliché in 'Amours de Voyage': powered by the conversational spring of the hexameter, its effect is refreshingly astringent.

Or bitter, according to taste. Clough did not publish 'Amours de Voyage' immediately. He knew it was too daring and perhaps too indelicate for its own immediate good, and he continued to fine-tune the text until 1858, when he allowed it to appear at a safe distance in an American journal, the *Atlantic Monthly*. However, in October 1849 he showed a first draft to a few friends, including John Shairp, a stout-hearted but strait-laced old Rugbeian, then a master at the school. Shairp's response is fascinating inasmuch as it demonstrates the type of attitude that Clough was up against: according to Shairp, a work of art that wasn't morally positive according to a narrow Christian definition could be of no worth or merit at all.

'The state of soul of which [the poem] is a projection I do not like,' Shairp complained. 'There is no hope, nor strength, nor belief... everything crumbles to dust beneath a ceaseless self-introspection and criticism... I would cast it behind me and the spirit from which it emanates and to higher, more healthful, hopeful things purely aspire... on the whole I regard "Les Amours" as your nature ridding itself of long-gathered bile.' To us, on the other hand, it is Clough's unflinching honesty – his refusal to be 'factitious' and pretend that everything fits, his determination to 'let the uncertainties remain uncertain' – which gives his writing its lasting stature.

***

Back in London, life turned out to be less simple than he had supposed. The optimism which had charged him in

1848 evaporated, as the liberal revolutions of that era faltered and failed and things got politically worse instead of better. The world was not ready for Clough – not his religious views, nor his hexameters either. He hated his job at University Hall and despised the idiots in charge. Although free from the tyranny of the 39 Articles, he now found himself under Unitarian masters who insisted on a session of morning prayers for the 11 students. To keep the peace, Clough wearily agreed to be present, although he refused either to lead them or to participate. The compromise was considered most unsatisfactory by all parties, and the smell of bad blood began to rise even higher after Clough refused to rusticate a student known to drink whisky and play cards. Apart from such incidents, the work consisted of an empty routine of disciplinary and administrative tasks, supplemented by a little teaching as Professor of English Literature, on a nugatory extra salary of £30 per annum. Since there was in fact virtually no serious study of English Literature at universities at the time (an exam paper set by Clough includes such intellectual challenges as 'Give the personal and professional pronouns as found in Chaucer'), the post was nominal and gave no joy. Thus his morale plummeted, and he sank into what his first biographer described as 'the dreariest and loneliest period of his life'.

The pressure of living in dank, stifling London did not

help. Nor did he much care for literary society, despite cordial new friendships with Carlyle and Thackeray and plenty of amusing invitations from those keen to lionise a well-reviewed young poet. He also continued an Oxford habit by breakfasting with Matthew Arnold every week, until Arnold found a wife and they drifted apart, Arnold privately fuming with exasperation at Clough's negativity and inability to make up his mind. 'You are too content to fluctuate,' Arnold told him, 'to be ever learning, never coming to the knowledge of the truth... you would never take your assiette [lot in life] as something determined final and unchangeable for you and proceed to work away on the basis of that: but were always poking and patching and cobbling...' The criticism hurt because it was justified. Clough became increasingly taciturn – as 'secret as an oyster', somebody put it – and in one letter he records how at a fashionable soirée: 'I was rather stupid and having caught sight of my face in a glass towards $^1/_2$ past 11, found myself so unutterably disagreeable that I was compelled to depart.'

The best advice he gave himself, he did not act on. To Shairp, in June 1850, he wrote: 'Let us not sit in a corner and think ourselves clever for our comfort, while the room is full of dancing and cheerfulness. The sum of the whole matter is this. Whatsoever your hand findeth to do, do it without fiddle-faddling.' But sit in a corner and fiddle-faddle he did. 'Nothing is very good, I am afraid, anywhere. I could have gone cracked at times last year with one thing or another, I think,' he wrote to Tom Arnold in May 1851, and there were moments when he felt close to breakdown.

Out of this state of mind came Clough's last major work, commonly known as 'Dipsychus'. Set in Venice, where he spent the summer of 1850, its form was influenced by the second part of Goethe's *Faust*, with scenes of dramatic dialogue that were intended for the mind's eye rather than literal theatrical performance. It focuses on Dipsychus ('split soul'), a modern young man of conscience and moral aspirations, haunted by a Mephistophelean spirit, who asks him why he bothers:

> Enjoy the minute
> And the substantial blessings in it
> Music and ice and evening air
> And all the sweets in perfect plenty
> Of the old *dolce far niente*.

Dipsychus tries to steer another higher course and to find some resolution:

> Seek, seeker, in thyself; submit to find
> In the stones bread and life in the blank mind.

But the Spirit pooh-poohs him with a rattling Gilbertian

jingle extolling the virtues of immediate gratification and the worldly wisdom of a little hypocrisy:

> I sit at my table *en grand seigneur*,
> And when I have done, toss a crust to the poor:
> Not only the pleasure, one self, of good living,
> But also the pleasure of now and then giving.
> So pleasant it is to have money, high-ho
> So pleasant it is to have money.

Chief of Dipsychus's temptations is sex. The attractions of Venice's parading prostitutes – like those of Oxford – bring him close to surrender. He recoils in horror:

> O weak weak fool! O God how quietly
> Out of our better into our worst selves
> Out of a true world which our reason knew
> Into a false world which our fancy makes
> We pass and never know – o weak weak fool.

'Well, if you don't wish, why, you don't,' retorts the Spirit.

> Leave it! But that's just why you won't.
> Come now! How many times per diem
> Are you not hankering to try 'em?

As Dipsychus struggles to take the view that sex should be reserved for 'the ancient holy course [of]… sweet domestic bonds/ The matrimonial sanctities', the Spirit paints an alluring and vivid picture of a prostitute's chamber, 'nicely fitted up for prayer... the calm Madonna o'er your head... where – as we said – *vous faites vôtre affaire* [you do your business]'. The Spirit doesn't win – Dipsychus can't just lie back and relax. But he doesn't lose either – Dipsychus never satisfactorily refutes his proposition.

Clough never finished 'Dipsychus', nor considered publishing it – for one thing, it would have been considered scandalously obscene, and it remains considerably more interesting as a biographical document than as a piece of literary art. Shairp's judgment that 'Amours de Voyage' was the result of 'your nature ridding itself of long-gathered bile' fits 'Dipsychus' much more accurately: both of them focus on a young man's intellectual fiddle-faddling, but the latter has none of the charm and ironic grace of 'Amours de Voyage', and there's something hysterical and compulsive about the way that it rambles on for so long, locked into the same 'Should-I? Why-shouldn't-you?' dialectic (as mentioned earlier, it finally breaks off with a prose epilogue, in which the poet and a fictitious uncle debate the merits and demerits of a Rugby education). 'Dipsychus' is the work of someone swimming against the tide through a deep mental crisis, and the effort seems to have been terminally exhausting. Effectively, it marks the end of Clough's career as a major poet.

***

Late in 1851, Clough left University Hall, after one of those all-too-familiar resignations to which the only alternative is the sack. Clough was not sorry to go, but found it difficult to know where to turn next. He had little money, a certain notoriety, and a streak of snobbish contempt for stupid people in high places. His options were therefore limited. First, he applied for a professorship in classics at the new university in Sydney. Shairp, who acted through this epoch as Clough's truth-teller, was adamantly opposed to the idea. 'No – you shan't. You with your confessedly unhard-fisted nature go to bluster and bully among gold-digging Australians. It must not be. Whatever there is defective in you, whatever stands between you and success here, will there tell tenfold against you… Your time will come, only bide it.' He was probably right about the mismatch, and fortunately Sydney turned Clough down, as did various other educational institutions closer to home, all frightened off by rumours of his religious views, or lack of them. Approaches were also made to several government departments, but in the days before competitive examinations made the civil service more meritocratic, secretarial positions were usually distributed on the recommendation of an aristocratic or otherwise empowered patron, something Clough – like all fiddle-faddlers, as stubborn as a mule – neither possessed nor deigned to cultivate.

What complicated the matter was Blanche Smith. Born in 1828 and nine years younger than Clough, she came from a well-to-do Home Counties family and was cousin on her mother's side to Florence Nightingale. He first met her in 1850 at a house party given by Richard Monckton Milnes, a Liberal MP of a literary bent, but their involvement with each other appears to date from 1851. Blanche was well educated by the standards of the day and quick to stand her ground – a quality that Clough's behaviour tested to the hilt.

Did he love her or didn't he? Did he want to marry her or didn't he? From the moment that they began their courtship, these questions fazed him. How could he commit to her, and what did that commitment imply? What was love, after all? He might love her now, but supposing in the future he should love someone else? 'Here in this dim deceitful misty moonshiny night-time of existence we grope about & run up against each other,' he wrote to her, in what must be the most poetically beautiful passage in all his letters, '& peer blindly but enquiringly into strange faces, and sooner or later (for comfort's sake for the night is cold, you see, & dreary) clasp hands & make vows & choose, & keep together – & withdraw again sometimes & wrench away hands, & seize others and do we know not what.' Behind it all, one suspects, was some guilt over a past love or even a shameful encounter to which he could not admit.

The result was that what should have made him happy only contributed to his anxiety, as can be seen from a correspondence which on his side amounts to a panic-stricken series of excuses and delaying tactics, often patronising ('my dear little child', he called her), some-times preachy, sometimes almost bullying. Elspie Mackaye had wanted to read what she pleased, when she pleased, but Clough forbade Blanche to read the 'atheistic' man-uscript of 'Dipsychus' when she found it in a trunk. However unfailing and unqualified her tolerance of him, he could not altogether open himself up, and his self-protectiveness became aggressive on occasion. 'You are very gentle sometimes,' she told him, 'but occasionally you scarify me.' How on earth did she bear it?

'I ask no girl to be my friend that we may be a fond foolish couple together all in all each to the other,' he wrote in January 1852. 'I will ask no one to put off her individuality for me; nor will I, weak and yielding as I am, if I can help it, put off mine for anyone. We are companions – fellow-labourers... But as for everlasting unions, and ties that no change can modify, do not dream of them.' Other letters attempt to suggest that the problem is hers rather than his: 'I cannot feel assurance in that I am more to you than a stage, a resting place. You are so young, you know, and really have not seen very many and various specimens of our kind.' Yet he could not let her go. Lonely as he was in London, he needed the intimacy of her patient acceptance and growing knowledge of his weaknesses as well as her quick, literate intelligence. In 'Amours de Voyage', Claude writes about Mary Trevellyn that

> ... she can talk in a rational way, can
> Speak upon subjects that really are matters of mind and of
> thinking
> Yet in perfection retain her simplicity ...

> She held me to nothing.
> No, I could talk as I pleased; come close; fasten ties, as I
> fancied;
> Bind and engage myself deep; - and lo, on the following
> morning
> It was all e'en as before, like losings in games played for
> nothing.

This was at the heart of Clough's attraction to Blanche too. (To be fair, it might also be noted that Mary takes a rather dimmer view of Claude:

> She that should love him must look for small love in return, –
> like the ivy

On the stone wall, must expect but a rigid and niggard
support, and
E'en to get that must go searching all round with her humble
embraces

– lines at which Blanche must have wryly nodded her
agreement. Clough may have known how trying he was,
though that scarcely excuses him.)

Slowly, two steps forward and one step back, the
relationship advanced to what the Victorians called an
'understanding' that they would eventually be married. It
was not an official engagement – something that Clough's
ultra-delicate scruples would not permit – and, at the
sensible insistence of Blanche's father, it was contingent
on an income of at least £600 per annum. This allowed
Clough a timely get-out clause. Given his aversion to
subscribing to the 39 Articles, most avenues of advancement were closed to him. If he was to remain in the
educational field for which he was qualified, he would have
to work in some more liberal climate. Having been turned
down by New South Wales, the best remaining option was
New England.

Enquiries to Emerson in Massachusetts elicited the
response that 'There is always teaching to be done here, to
any extent, at all prices,' as well as the freelance literary
and lecturing labours that he himself undertook. 'I think

your card... a very safe one,' he concluded, and Clough decided that he would play it.

Poor Blanche! 'Do you *really* think it would be *good* for us to part?' she pleaded. The idea was that she would come over to join him when he had established himself, but there was an element of vagueness as to his intentions. 'Let us be content and wait,' he enjoined her. And so in November 1852 Clough returned to the land of his childhood. His mood was more optimistic than it had been since he first left Oxford: he had his liberty, plenty of potentially useful introductions and the promise of Emerson's help and friendship. Most of all, he relished the prospect of living somewhere he would not constantly be pressed to declare his beliefs, among people less 'churchy' and more freethinking than the British.

Or so he thought. Once in Boston, he found it a good deal less idyllic than he had anticipated. He missed Blanche dreadfully and wrote to her almost daily, listing the most trivial events at a tedious length which suggests his loneliness. Although furnished with excellent references and introductions, he did not find either work or friends easily. Relations with Emerson were strained by the louring presence of Emerson's silent neurasthenic wife. Polite literary society proved predominantly Unitarian; elsewhere the eccentric religious notions and superstitions (Clough describes them as 'rococo'), including the contemporary vogue for spiritualist table-tapping, irritated his rationality. He was sceptical of the Yankee version of democracy and the burning cause of Abolition ('I should be a Free Soiler, which only means that you won't have any new slave states,' he explained to Blanche). Worst of all, he complained fastidiously, were the terrible domestic servants – 'dirty, uninstructed Irish, who are very slow in learning to be clean, and very quick in learning to be independent'.

All this made his first transatlantic months miserable. He picked up bits and pieces of teaching and translating, but his earnings were far from the sum required for the blessing of Blanche's father. He blew hot and cold over the idea of opening a school, possibly on Rugbeian lines. Yet by April 1853 he could tell Blanche that he was 'very comfortably settled and on very easy terms with the American world in general'. He had met a new soulmate in the art historian and intellectual Charles Eliot Norton; he found America 'hopeful' in a way that England wasn't; and he felt that, given a little more time, he could establish himself to the point at which Blanche could marry him and emigrate.

But several interested parties in England were busily pulling other strings. A change of government meant that Carlyle's great friend Lady Ashburton was now in a position to call in some favours from cabinet ministers.

The result was that Clough was offered a secure civil service job as examiner in the Education Office at an annual salary of £300, with good prospects of promotion. At the same time, his old friend Frederick Temple offered him the Vice-Principalship of a teacher-training college at a salary of £400. After much toing and froing too tedious to relate, Clough placated Mr Smith and accepted the examinership. He did not really want to come home, but he submitted. It was another defeat, and one from which he never recovered.

In June 1853 he returned to England, and a year later finally married Blanche Smith. Few details of their relatively brief life together survive, but there is no reason to think that they were positively or personally unhappy. Their first child, a boy, died within hours of his birth in 1855; three years later came Florence, followed by Arthur, in whose infant company Clough took great paternal pleasure. Without much money to spare, they lived in St Mark's Crescent in Primrose Hill and Campden Hill Road, Kensington – not then the smart areas they have latterly become. Occasionally, he saw Tennyson, Carlyle and old Oxford friends. But about this aspect of Clough's life there is little else to say. Of how his confused feelings for Blanche resolved themselves; of any inner turmoil, sexual, religious or ethical; of a creative or intellectual demon driving him on, there is absolutely no evidence.

He seems, if not lobotomised, then tranquillised. His letters, chiefly to his American friends like the sympathetic Charles Eliot Norton, are weary and *distrait*, little more than polite hearsay reports on current affairs and new books. 'I fear I read nothing myself', he wrote, 'except the occasional newspaper.'

Clough's work in Whitehall does not seem to have been strenuous. From 11am until 5pm, he assessed the reports of school inspectors (one of whom was Matthew Arnold) and set and supervised examinations for teachers. In 1856, in the wake of the debacle in the Crimea, he travelled to France, Austria and Prussia, where he spent three months researching their superior system of military education. In 1858 he was promoted to the rank of Private Secretary to the Vice-President of the Privy Council Committee on Education. At least the question of his views of the incarnation and resurrection did not arise: this was down-to-earth work of the sort that Rugby approved.

Whatever literary ambitions he had once cherished now faded. Eventually he completed the project, begun in Boston, of translating Plutarch's *Lives*, and wrote a long review of a new edition of Goethe's ballads for *Fraser's* magazine. In 1858 he was pleased to receive the only money he would earn from poetry in his lifetime, when 'Amours de Voyage' was finally published in the *Atlantic Monthly*. Yet over all these settled years in London he produced nothing new. Clough was never a dreamer or an idealist, but as he approached his 40th birthday, some vital flow of hope was draining away from his life.

What sprung up to fill the spiritual vacuum was the cause of someone described by Elizabeth Gaskell as standing alone, 'halfway between God and his creatures': Blanche's formidable cousin, Florence Nightingale. Obeying an inner spiritual voice but dismissive of conventional Christianity, this fearless and invincible woman was engaged in playing the entire male establishment at a brilliant political game which she had every intention of winning, at any cost. Clough was vital to her strategy – one of her pawns, but also one of her bishops, sent out across the board on small errands and large missions while she herself remained physically immobile and closeted.

Clough first met her through Blanche's mother in the early 1850s. Witty, energetic, attractive and well-connected, she was much courted, much admired, and, had she so chosen, she could have enjoyed a conventional female destiny of a comfortable, even luxurious kind. Instead, she set to work, investigating sanitary and hospital conditions throughout Europe and composing a tract aimed at satisfying the religious needs of 'intelligent artisans'. What motivated her was a craving for power and influence, and it extended to the personal affairs of her quiet and pretty younger cousin. In particular, Florence interfered significantly – and benevolently – in the vacillations which preceded Blanche's engagement to Clough. She even worked out elaborate budgets detailing the expenditure they would require in order to set up a married home, calculated in relation to the statistically probable number of children they would produce. Such labours were not wasted: Blanche's mother venerated Florence, and her support for Clough's case must have swayed the family's arguments. Initially, however, Clough found her somewhat frightening – aggressive and 'arithmetical', with a waspish wit and a cold eye, she seemed a far cry from the fresh, sunny girls he fancied.

But after he returned from America, she mesmerised him, like a rabbit stunned by a bright light. She was magnificently convinced, focused, imperious – everything that he wasn't. Her theological reflections were brisk: Dr Arnold would have approved of their practicality. God, she thought, did not intend us to hang about. The injunction 'Wait on the Lord – Wait patiently on him' was ridiculous. 'If I did not believe that God was working out a scheme in which I myself was taking part,' she scoffed, 'I could give up working altogether.' 'We are not meant for servants, set to look after so many pairs of sheets, but for something much higher,' she continued in the course of one blazing conversation recorded by Clough. 'If God were to say to me "Well done good & faithful servant" – I should be very much surprised.'

There was nothing romantic or even particularly intimate about their relationship (she always addressed him, with formal propriety, as 'Mr Clough'). What Florence Nightingale required was help, not sympathy, and she had no compunction about demanding it. There were places from which her sex debarred her. She needed men to serve as agents, spies and mouthpieces; men who could represent her in the exclusively male forums of government and decision-making. The deeply pious and gentle-natured Earl of Pembroke, Sidney Herbert, a minister in Palmerston's government, was her chief ally. Clough did not walk the corridors of power, but he was of use in other more mundane respects, and she took full advantage of the passivity which characterised his obstinate integrity. Beset by his own uncertainties and fiddle-faddle, Clough found salvation in someone else's decisiveness.

In 1854 he had escorted her to Calais, en route for Scutari and the appalling military hospitals of the Crimean War. After more than two years of astonishing achievement in conditions of unimaginable horror, she returned to England, broken in health but indomitable, and frenzied with a sense that her work had only just begun. Under Herbert's chairmanship, a royal commission was set up to investigate matters relating to the health of the British army; and to its members, Florence Nightingale would deliver a massive 800-page report, composed of her own experiences and observations, buttressed by impregnable columns of figures, statistics and tabulations. In the words of Lytton Strachey, 'Her desire for work could now scarcely be distinguished from mania.' Plagued by one of those weirdly vague collections of nervous symptoms to which Victorian ladies were so prone, she was often confined to her bedroom for months at a time, announcing to visitors that she was dying. Not that it seemed to make the slightest difference either to her industry or her capacity to command and cajole and research and dictate; but the dreadful prospect of this national heroine's imminent demise stimulated members of her retinue to redouble their efforts to do her bidding.

Clough's central function in the grand plan was to serve as secretary to the Nightingale Fund, a charity set up to promote the proper training of nurses. Given his relatively easy load in Whitehall, this was something he could properly manage. But the cause did not stop there. It also involved the minute proofreading of the report and the verifying of facts behind its assertions; there were timetables to consult, packages to be wrapped and dispatched, letters to be dictated. Clough was less partner or deputy than courier, errand-boy, 'cab-horse'. 'If you have any commissions, pray consider me,' he wrote to her once. It was an invitation she accepted all too literally, calling on him at all hours of the day or night, without regard for his comfort, privacy or recreation. The matter may have been the smallest point of detail, but it could never wait – she required his immediate attention, she required his presence, and, out of some sense of duty or self-punishment, he answered her call. 'Blessed is he who has found his work; let him ask no other blessedness,' wrote Carlyle in *Past and Present*. Rugbeian that he was, Clough had long believed in the truth of that beatitude.

***

It is easy to mock, and literary intellectuals have always seen Clough's relationship with Florence Nightingale as the climax of his tragedy and the emasculation of his genius. Yet it is of a piece, one might say, with the rest of his life. He would not have regarded his enslavement as an aberration, let alone a betrayal of his best self and its aspirations: he was serving something greater than his own talent, and, it is reasonable to argue, as he himself doubtless would have, that Florence Nightingale's reforms did more material, quantifiable good to humankind than any number of poems. If one thinks of the false gods to whom 20th-century writers of even greater genius than Clough dedicated themselves, then his choice becomes even finer. There were emotional tugs as well: Florence Nightingale was capable of outbursts of heart-rending gratitude. She could be extravagantly generous – in 1858, she helped him over a financial hump by giving him without fuss or question, £500, the equivalent of a full year's salary ('If I could give him £10,000 a year, it would be a poor acknowledgement of what he has done for us,' she wrote) – and she was always deeply attached to Clough's wife and children. (Some charming letters survive, recording her pleasure in Clough's infant son, whom she seems to have had staying with her. 'Arty, the little chaps', she coos, was 'the most beautifully organised little piece of humanity I ever saw'.)

Nevertheless, there was a price to be paid. It wasn't just the work which was exhausting; Clough also bore the full force of Florence Nightingale's morbid belief that her death was imminent. She discussed her funeral with him, she rewrote her will, and, on one gruesome occasion, she made him sit while she wrote a series of 'last' letters to be delivered after she had passed away. Nor was she even-tempered: without shouting or losing control, she could also be vilely irascible and witheringly contemptuous. Her rages were easily provoked. To others, she accused Clough of laziness and lack of true zeal, and one imagines there were occasions when he felt the stinging lash of her scorpion tongue.

When Clough's own health collapsed late in 1859, it was as though he had taken the mantle of her illness upon himself. He had never been sickly. He was physically active – an inexhaustible walker, an enthusiastic swimmer. By the standards of the day, his constitution was robust, and, apart from some rheumatic complaints, whatever illness he had suffered in adolescence seems to have been psychosomatic and depressive rather than genuinely physical. But, for the last two years of his life, he fell victim to a form of 'nervous breakdown' which steadily depleted his resources. It is difficult to discern through the vague medical vocabulary of the day a precise pathological history, but we know from Blanche's letters that the slide in his health started with a bad attack of scarlatina, 'after which I think he returned to work too soon'. Then came 'an accident to his foot... which weakened him and shattered his nerves very much'. Another blow was the death of his mother from a paralytic stroke. 'But though these I believe hastened his decline, I can hardly think they did more. It was pure overwork which exhausted his brain and left no strength to stand against the final attack.' The Education Office gave him unpaid leave; whether Florence Nightingale – thumping the drums at a crucial moment in her campaign – left him alone is not known. He spent two months in the spa town of Malvern, taking Dr Manby Gully's water-cure, a fad of the time. Still very weak, he talked of a trip to America, as far away from it all as it was possible to be, but his eventual destination was the Isle of Wight, where he spent six happy weeks at Freshwater en famille. 'Our children are growing big little things,' writes Blanche with the touching naiveté that characterises her letters. 'The baby runs about and digs on the shore and is a great amusement to his Papa, and Florence is a chatterbox of the first water.' The Tennysons were 'kind and pleasant neighbours', with 'two nice boys of 7 and 9 who patronise Florence to her heart's content'.

In April 1861, a longer convalescence was ordered, and Clough sailed to Greece and Constantinople. Blanche, now pregnant, stayed at home with the children. En route, he was inspired to begin some new poetry for the first time in almost a decade.

'Mari Magno' ('On the Open Sea') is a nautical Victorian version of *The Canterbury Tales*, in which a group of passengers on a transatlantic packet while away the days by telling each other curious and occasionally risqué stories on the theme of marriage. Rattling along in a light rhyming patter of no great linguistic density or subtlety ('prose written in verse' said one critic), 'Mari Magno' seems to have been written for Clough's private amusement. It is amateur poetry, prolix and unpolished, the work of a convalescing civil servant, but not without its doggerel charm:

My uncle lived the mountain o'er,
A rector and a bachelor;
The vicarage was by the sea,
That was the home of Emily...

Over the ensuing months, he would continue to add to the manuscript, and at some points, as we shall see, he found that what he was writing struck a deeper emotional note.

Greece he enjoyed, but once he arrived in the sweltering alien heat of Constantinople he became violently home-sick and made immediately for home. After three weeks, it became clear that he was still unwell and that London was the worst place for him.

'He overdid himself instantly not by what he did but by the old anxieties coming back to him,' explained Blanche to a friend. His sick-leave was extended yet again and Blanche firmly arranged for someone else to take over the secretaryship of the Nightingale Fund. Clough went to France this time, with the notion that Blanche would join him as soon as she was safely delivered of her baby. Via Paris, he made for the Auvergne and the Pyrenees, where the Tennysons were based for the summer. They were pleasant, undemanding people, and Clough enjoyed their company. One night he wrote another episode of 'Mari Magno', entitled 'The Clergyman's Second Tale'.

Edward and Jane were married at 21:

> And fonder she of him or he of her
> Were hard to say.

After nine years of hard work in an insurance office, Edward collapses and takes sick-leave. At his wife's urging, he goes off to recuperate on the Continent and, in a hotel, he falls for the charms of a fellow-guest who sits opposite him, like the girl in the train in 'Natura Naturans'. Electrified by mutual desire, they consummate a brief but torrid affair, which Edward guiltily terminates when he receives a letter from Jane and their daughter. He confesses all to his wife, but, although he recovers his health and goes back to work, he cannot face returning home. Instead he begins an intense penance, meeting his wife only once every three months to hand over his earnings. One evening, he is followed by a 'poor flaunting creature of the town'. It is the woman from the hotel, fallen to prostitution. This time, however, he manages to resist her siren call – watching her slink off into the 'gas-lit darkness', he reflects that 'it was hell, and he some unblest wanderer there'. Back in his lodgings, he receives a telegram from his wife, informing him that their daughter has been taken dangerously ill. Now he finds that he has the moral strength to go back to them. Jane, who believes:

> ... in one who takes away
> Our sin and gives us righteousness instead

freely grants him forgiveness, asking whether it can be right to leave her as a single mother while he flagellates himself with remorse for a sin which he has expiated. Edward relents, the daughter recovers, and the family resumes its former happy life. The complex autobiographical resonance of this story, with its element of conventionally Victorian Christian morality, needs no emphasis.

Years later, Tennyson recalled how one evening in the Pyrenees, Clough had read them part of 'Mari Magno' and broken down in tears – the only time he is ever recorded as showing any such emotion. We cannot be sure that it was 'The Clergyman's Second Tale' which thus unmanned him, but it is hard to doubt it.

Whatever the connection, Clough's last letters confirm that, like Edward, he was lonely and wanted to come home. 'I think it very funny of you', he wrote sourly to Blanche, 'to suppose that it can be so very pleasant or easily endurable to stay poking out abroad for more than two or three months at a time, all by oneself or something no better – or perhaps worse.' And there was another anxiety to contend with: after a long decline marked by the same sort of lingering breakdown that Clough was enduring, Sidney Herbert had died – his last words reportedly being 'Poor Florence! Our joint work… unfinished… tried to do.' Florence Nightingale was duly devastated at the loss of her right-hand man and chief ally in government, and Clough must have been haunted by the knowledge that she would be feeling failed and deserted too. She was the one who was meant to be dying, yet she was the only one to fight on. How could Clough sleep quietly with that sentence pounding in his head? But Blanche's letters implored him to stay where he was: the stress, the 'associations and return to old thoughts', the risk of 'being dragged into what you don't foresee' and exposed to the demands of 'the Fund and Flo', would exacerbate his symptoms.

In September, a baby girl called Blanche Athena was safely delivered and dispatched – as was the Victorian fashion – to the tender care of a wet nurse. As soon as she was able, Blanche went out to France to join her restless husband. Together they travelled by train and diligence through Switzerland and the Italian lakes, intending to work their way south and reach Rome before the winter. In Florence, Clough managed a day or two of sightseeing and shopping – they went to look at the Baptistry and Clough bought Blanche a copy of Dante's *Divina Commedia*. Then he collapsed again. For the next few weeks his condition steadily worsened, and he appears to have suffered a stroke. 'It was a regular low malaria fever,' wrote Blanche, 'but when that subsided it showed the weakness beneath the worn-out brain. Symptoms of paralysis came on – in the eye – in one leg. He became wandering but not very much so ever and never painfully. Just at the last it was paralysis of the lungs... he was always very like himself – very gentle – and even in his wanderings so natural. It was only as if his thoughts were running away with him, running into each other a little.'

By now, it had become clear that he was dying. His sister Annie arrived from England, and he had just enough strength to recognise her. In a moment of lucidity, he asked Blanche for a pencil and wrote four lines. As she recalled: 'He took hold of my two hands in his & said, "My hands are whiter than yours now." I said, "Because you've been ill, dear." He said very quietly, "Yes dear I know that." He seemed more at ease when his verses were done. I copied them out & told him but he began again thinking of his poems before long...'

Blanche then scribbled a plea to the Education Office to beg them to allow him more leave – but the letter was never sent, for, within hours of her writing it, 42-year-old Arthur Hugh Clough was dead. After a cast was taken of his head and hand, he was buried in a simple grave in Florence's Protestant cemetery, 'a very nice little place – where the tall cypresses stand against that beautiful blue sky and the hills look down on it'. Blanche was brave, but desolate. 'Sometimes I think the misery is greater than I can bear, and that if grief could kill one, I ought to have died before this... I feel so alone,' she confessed a couple of weeks later in a letter breaking the news to Charles Eliot Norton, 'though two or three most touching and comforting letters have come to me. I do think many know what he was, and though he did so little that will show, he left a seed in the hearts of many.'

The letters of condolence and obituary notices struck the note of unfulfilled promise and wrong turnings which would become the staple of all memories of Clough. 'He always seemed to me to have his voice choked by his own fulness and by his conscientiousness, besides his too great modesty,' wrote Francis Newman, John Henry's brother, to Blanche. Frederick Temple, an old Balliol friend, now Headmaster of Rugby and later a great Archbishop of Canterbury, went further: 'He seemed to me when I first knew him, the ablest and greatest man I had ever come across, and the one from whom I had learned more than from any other man I know.' For many, the loss was more personal: even if Clough was neither warm nor open, he was unfailingly gentle and sincere and, however exasperating his refusals and hesitations, he had no enemies. Tom Arnold, probably the man with whom Clough was most emotionally intimate, put it with heartfelt simplicity: 'I loved and looked up to him more than any other.' Tom's brother Matthew took a cooler view. 'He is one of the few people who ever made a deep impression upon me,' he wrote to his mother, 'and as time goes on, and one finds no one else who makes such an impression, one's feeling about those who did make it gets to be something more and more distinct and unique. Besides', he added tartly, 'the object of it no longer survives to wear it out [by] becoming ordinary and different from what he was.'

There was gossip, too, in the wake of a death following so soon upon the similar collapse of Sidney Herbert. 'I hardly know whether it lessens the pang of his loss', continued Francis Newman in his letter to Blanche, 'to be told (as I *have* been told) that the fatal weakness of the brain was induced by overwork in the cause of Florence Nightingale and her benign plans. Alas, one cannot be satisfied that one martyrdom should entail another.'

The martyr herself was long in writing to Blanche. The letter which eventually came was fervent with compassion: 'Do not my dear Blanche suppose that, because I have been silent, I have not felt, always as now, deeply now as ever, at every waking hour, night & day, the greatness of her [viz. Blanche's] loss & how immeasurably greater hers than any one's. How well he loved you, who knew better than I? Indeed I know no husband's love greater than his. What he was, I knew; & therefore what his love must have been. For the greater the soul, the greater the love. You have been like Mary at the foot of the cross…'

Later, she did not deny a degree of culpability for his

early demise. 'Seeing the blundering harasses which were the uses to which we put him, he seemed like a race-horse harnessed to a coal-truck,' she admitted in that scoffing tone which was the essence of her *terribilità*. But it did not deter her and, for all her complaints, she would not die until 1910.

In 1869 Blanche edited a volume of her husband's *Poems and Prose Remains*, including much unpublished verse and a discreet memoir. Acting as a good Victorian widow, she exercised a firm censoring pencil over the sexual content of his work, and the critics in the quarterlies preferred to talk of its author as 'a soul "perplexed in the extreme", yet hopefully and devoutly believing in God and duty'. Thus began the consolidation of the two-dimensional picture of Clough, already adumbrated in Matthew Arnold's elegy 'Thyrsis', a lament for those golden student days in Oxford, which dramatises Arnold's belief that Clough had needlessly knotted himself up in doubt and – as it were – dropped out, unable to take the strain:

> What though the music of thy rustic flute
> Kept not for long its happy, country tone,
> Lost it too soon, and learnt a stormy note
> Of men contention-tost, of men who groan,
> Which task'd thy pipe too sore, and tired thy throat –

It fail'd and thou wast mute;
Yet hadst thou always visions of our light,
And long with men of care thou couldst not stay,
And soon thy foot resumed its wandering way
Left human haunt, and on alone till night.

Fifty years later, and this feebleness was diagnosed as symptomatic of a disease of the era. To Lytton Strachey's sharp eye – in *Eminent Victorians*, a book for a post-First World War generation ready to mock their fathers' gods – Clough's problem was described as an obsession with 'nothing but moral good, moral evil, moral influence and moral responsibility' that finally wore him out and left him 'conscientiously doing up brown-paper parcels for Florence Nightingale'. But Strachey squinted. His iconoclastic agenda prevented him from seeing that Clough was in a sense on his side – someone of a profoundly liberal intellectual temperament, sensitive to grey ethical shades and reluctant to pass judgment, lacking in piety and unfailing in honesty. Today, we should be ready for Clough: his virtues are those prized by our own tottering culture, and he speaks to us clearly, without front. As one modern critic has written: 'No other 19th-century poet stands so nakedly before posterity' – a tribute which would have made this most modest of men blush, even though he knew it in his heart to be deserved.

ACKNOWLEDGEMENTS

This monograph has benefited from consultation of the collections of Clough's writings held in the libraries of Rugby School, the Bodleian and Balliol College, Oxford. My grateful thanks go to all the librarians concerned, especially Dr Penelope Bulloch at Balliol. I would also like to thank Robert Gray for his useful comments; and Kate Christiansen for her sterling help with preliminary research.

SELECT BIBLIOGRAPHY

The major editions of Clough's work are published by Oxford University Press: *The Correspondence of Arthur Hugh Clough*, ed. Frederick L. Mulhauser (1957), 2 vols; *The Poems of Arthur Hugh Clough*, ed. Frederick L. Mulhauser (1974); and *The Oxford Diaries of Arthur Hugh Clough*, ed. Anthony Kenny (1990).

The two major modern biographical studies, also published by OUP, are those of Katharine Chorley, *Arthur Hugh Clough: The Uncommitted Mind* (1962) and R. K. Biswas, *Arthur Hugh Clough: Towards a Reconsideration* (1972).

Rupert Christiansen is the author of Prima Donna, Romantic Affinities, Tales of the New Babylon *and* The Visitors. *He is opera critic for* The Daily Telegraph *and writes regularly for* Opera, The Spectator *and* Harpers & Queen. *A Fellow of the Royal Society of Literature, he lives in London.*